Wheels, Wings, and Water

Cars

Heather Miller

Heinemann Library
Chicago, Illinois

a division of Reed Elsevier Inc.
Chicago, Illinois

Customer Service 888-454-2279
Visit our website at www.heinemannlibrary.com

Designed by Sue Emerson, Heinemann Library; Page layout by Que-Net Media
Printed and bound in the United States by Lake Book Manufacturing, Inc.
Photo research by Amor Montes De Oca

07 06 05 04 03
10 9 8 7 6 5 4 3 2 1

Library of Congress Cataloging-in-Publication Data
Miller, Heather.
Cars / Heather Miller.
v. cm. – (Wheels, wings, and water)
Includes index.
Contents: What are cars? – What do cars look like? – What are cars made of? – How did cars look long ago? – What is a sedan? – What is a minivan? – What is a convertible? – What is a sports car? – What are some special cars? – Quiz – Picture glossary.
ISBN 1-4034-0880-7 (HC), 1-4034-3619-3 (Pbk.)
1. Automobiles–Juvenile literature. [1. Automobiles.] I. Title. II. Series.
TL147.M55 2003
629.222–dc21
2002014722

Acknowledgments
The author and publishers are grateful to the following for permission to reproduce copyright material:
p. 4 Michael Newman/PhotoEdit, Inc.; p. 5 PhotoDisc; pp. 6L, 12 Jane Faircloth/Transparencies, Inc.; p. 6R Kim Sayer/Corbis; pp. 7, 19, 22, 24 Jeff Greenberg/Visuals Unlimited, Inc.; p. 8 David Turnley/Corbis; p. 9 Science VU/Visuals Unlimited, Inc.; p. 10 Ken Stepnell/Bruce Coleman, Inc.; p. 11 Visuals Unlimited; p. 13 Tom and Dee Ann McCarthy/Corbis; p. 14 Don Mason/Corbis; p. 15 David Young-Wolff/PhotoEdit, Inc.; p. 16 Ellen Faircloth/Transparencies, Inc.; p. 17 J. E. Glenn/Transparencies, Inc.; p. 18 Spectrum/Robertstock.com; p. 20 D. Maybury/TRIP; p. 21 Vic Bider/Index Stock Imagery Inc.; p. 23 row 1 (L-R) Visuals Unlimited, Jeff Greenberg/Visuals Unlimited, Inc., Science VU/Visuals Unlimited, Inc.; row 2 (L-R) Michael Waine/Corbis, EyeWire, Owaki-Kulla/Corbis; row 3 (L-R) Science VU/Visuals Unlimited, Inc., Stephanie Maze/Corbis, Michael Newman/PhotoEdit, Inc.; row 4 Jeff Greenberg/Visuals Unlimited; back cover (L-R) Science VU/Visuals Unlimited, Inc., EyeWire

Cover photograph by Richard Hamilton Smith/Corbis

Special thanks to our advisory panel for their help in the preparation of this book:

Alice Bethke, Library Consultant
Palo Alto, CA

Eileen Day, Preschool Teacher
Chicago, IL

Kathleen Gilbert,
Second Grade Teacher
Round Rock, TX

Sandra Gilbert,
Library Media Specialist
Fiest Elementary School
Houston, TX

Jan Gobeille,
Kindergarten Teacher
Garfield Elementary
Oakland, CA

Angela Leeper,
Educational Consultant
North Carolina Department
of Public Instruction
Wake Forest, NC

Some words are shown in bold, **like this.**
You can find them in the picture glossary on page 23.

Contents

What Are Cars? 4
What Do Cars Look Like? 6
What Are Cars Made Of? 8
How Did Cars Look Long Ago? 10
What Is a Sedan? 12
What Is a Minivan? 14
What Is a Convertible? 16
What Is a Sports Car? 18
What Are Some Special Cars? 20
Quiz 22
Picture Glossary 23
Note to Parents and Teachers 24
Answer to Quiz 24
Index 24

What Are Cars?

A car is a **vehicle** with four wheels.

Cars can carry people and things.

Engines make cars go.

People wear **seat belts** to stay safe.

What Do Cars Look Like?

Cars can be almost any color.

Cars can be small or large.

Some car **headlights** are shaped like **circles.**

Some car windows are shaped like **rectangles** or **squares.**

What Are Cars Made Of?

Most cars are made of metal.

The tires are made of rubber.

The **dashboard** of this car is plastic.

The seats are covered with cloth.

How Did Cars Look Long Ago?

Early cars looked like **carriages.**

The driver moved a stick to steer the car.

Later, cars had doors and windows.

These cars had **steering wheels.**

What Is a Sedan?

A sedan is a car with four doors.

Sedans have front and back seats.

Many sedans can carry four people.

They have **trunks** to hold things.

What Is a Minivan?

A minivan looks like a small truck.

Minivans can carry many people and things.

Some minivans have a front, middle, and back seat.

They have long, sliding doors, too.

What Is a Convertible?

A convertible has a top that can fold down.

The driver pushes a button to make the top move.

If it starts to rain, the driver puts up the top.

What Is a Sports Car?

Sports cars are small cars.

Many sports cars have only two seats.

Some sports cars can go very fast!

What Are Some Special Cars?

Race cars go very fast.

They drive on **racetracks.**

Limousines are very long cars.

Many people can ride in a limousine.

Quiz

Do you know what kind of car this is?

Can you find it in the book?

Look for the answer on page 24.

Picture Glossary

carriage
page 10

headlight
page 7

rectangle
page 7

steering wheel
page 11

circle
page 7

limousine
page 21

seat belt
page 5

trunk
page 13

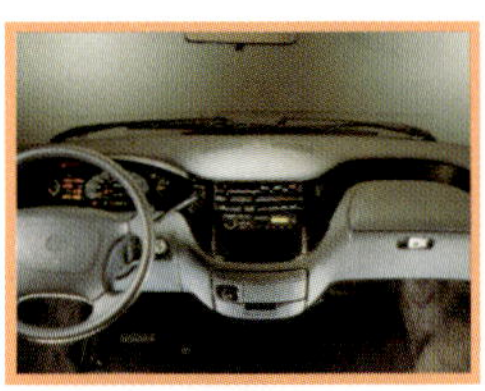

dashboard
page 9

racetrack
page 20

square
page 7

vehicle
page 4

engine
page 5

Note to Parents and Teachers

Reading for information is an important part of a child's literacy development. Learning begins with a question about something. Help children think of themselves as investigators and researchers by encouraging their questions about the world around them. Each chapter in this book begins with a question. Read the question together. Talk about what you think the answer might be. Read the text to find out if your predictions were correct. Think of other questions you could ask about the topic, and discuss where you might find the answers. In this book, the picture glossary symbol for vehicle is a car. Explain to children that a vehicle is something that can move people or things from one place to another. Some vehicles have motors, like cars, but others do not.

Index

convertible 16–17
dashboard. 9
engine 5
headlights. 7
limousine. 21
racecar 20
seat belts 5
seats. 9, 12, 15, 18
sedan. 12–13
sports car 18–19
tires. 8
trunk 13
wheels 4, 10–11
windows 7, 11

Answer to quiz on page 22

This is a sports car.